STATIONS OF THE CROSS FOR THE SICK & SUFFERING

ADAPTED FROM

STATIONS OF THE CROSS FOR SHUT-INS

BY

MARGARET R. CONNELLY

BOOKS & MEDIA
BOSTON

Nihil Obstat:
John G. Hogan

Imprimatur:
† Richard Cardinal Cushing

Adapted from *Stations of the Cross for Shut-Ins* by Margaret R. Connelly.

ISBN 0-8198-6991-0

http://www.pauline.org

E-mail: PBM_EDIT@INTERRAMP.COM

Illustrations:
Original works of various painters from the second half of the nineteenth century (1870-1890)
Roman School of painting of Via Margutta
Parish Church of S. Giacomo in Augusta, Rome

Photos:
Franco Marzi and Carla Morselli

Printed and published in the U.S.A. by Pauline Books & Media, 50 St. Paul's Avenue, Boston, MA 02130.

Pauline Books & Media is the publishing house of the Daughters of St. Paul, an international congregation of women religious serving the Church with the communications media.

1 2 3 4 5 99 98 97 96

Introductory Prayer

JESUS, MY LOVING SAVIOR, I offer this way of the cross to you and I unite my sufferings to yours in reparation for my many sins and offenses.

Through these stations I can enter in a small way into your bitter passion and death. Lord, I am sorry for the part my sins have played in your sufferings. As I make the way of the cross and meditate on your passion, I hope to grow in love for you and others. Please give me a heartfelt sorrow for my sins.

Now I am suffering from an illness. Help me to profit from this time of sickness and use it for my spiritual growth. I join my prayers with those who are suffering all over the world. *Amen.*

A plenary indulgence is attached to the practice of the way of the cross, providing that the other general conditions for gaining plenary indulgences are fulfilled: detachment from all sin, sacramental confession and Communion, and prayer for the intentions of the Holy Father. To gain the indulgence, the way of the cross should be made before legitimately erected stations, moving from one station to another. However, those who are impeded from making the way of the cross can gain the same indulgence by dedicating at least a half hour to devout reading and meditation on the passion and death of our Lord Jesus Christ (cf. *Manual of Indulgences,* Vatican Edition, 1968, n. 63).

FIRST STATION
Jesus Is Condemned to Death

We adore you, O Christ, and we bless you, because by your holy cross you have redeemed the world.

JESUS, MY KING, I see the sufferings you endure as you stand before Pilate, awaiting the death sentence. Your sufferings from the night before, beginning with the agony in Gethsemane, have left their mark on you. You were abused and humiliated, but you did not respond with anger or hate. You asked forgiveness for your enemies and now you accept Pilate's decree of death for you.

I know that one day I too will die. I pray that I may recover from this illness and spend my strength in serving you. Help me to accept this time of sickness in a way that will bring me closer to you. I also pray for all those people suffering from terminal diseases, that they may spend their last days sustained by your loving care.

Our Father, Hail Mary, Glory to the Father. Have mercy on us, O Lord, have mercy on us.

SECOND STATION
Jesus Carries His Cross

We adore you, O Christ, and we bless you, because by your holy cross you have redeemed the world.

LORD JESUS, my heart aches for you when I consider how you bear the heavy cross on your shoulders and take the first steps toward Calvary.

You are sick and fatigued from the merciless scourging. Blood from your thorn-crowned head blinds you, and the heavy cross tears open the flesh on your shoulder. Jesus, I venerate the wound on your shoulder with a prayer from St. Bernard:

"Loving Jesus, gentle Lamb of God, I honor that most painful wound of your shoulder, where you bore the heavy cross that tore your flesh and exposed the bones. It caused you more pain than any other wound in your holy body. I adore you, Jesus, and I praise you. I thank you for this most sacred and painful wound, asking you by that searing pain and the burden of the cross to be merciful to me, a sinner. Forgive all my sins, and lead me toward heaven along the way of the cross."

Our Father, Hail Mary, Glory to the Father. Have mercy on us, O Lord, have mercy on us.

THIRD STATION

Jesus Falls the First Time

We adore you, O Christ, and we bless you, because by your holy cross you have redeemed the world.

LORD JESUS, this station brings home to me how much you suffered for us! After enduring a night of agony, you now begin the journey to Calvary. You soon fall beneath the weight of the cross. Blood trickles down from your head and into your eyes. So often, your eyes had looked with compassion on the sick and the suffering. Now, your persecutors look on you with hate and scorn.

Loving Savior, what made you endure all this for us? You did it out of your infinite love. You carried the weight of our sins, a far greater burden than the wood of the cross.

Jesus, I am sorry for all my sins. I offer my sufferings in union with yours. In particular, I pray for all those who are struggling to break a habit of sin.

Our Father, Hail Mary, Glory to the Father. Have mercy on us, O Lord, have mercy on us.

FOURTH STATION

Jesus Meets Mary, His Mother

We adore you, O Christ, and we bless you, because by your holy cross you have redeemed the world.

O Mary, my dear Mother, my heart is filled with sorrow for you when I meditate on this fourth station. You can only watch as your son Jesus passes by, dragging the heavy cross. He stumbles on alone, since his friends have deserted him. You must want to run toward him, embrace him and help him carry the cross. But the soldiers would not allow it. You want to be as close to Jesus as you can, and watch him to the end.

Mary, how hard it is for you to see your son suffer and die! When Jesus was an infant, you had wrapped him in swaddling clothes, but now you see him covered with blood and wounds. You can only look at him with a heart overflowing with love. Mary, pray for all mothers who have to suffer the death of a son or daughter. Comfort them in their grief and give them the inner strength to grow through the pain.

Our Father, Hail Mary, Glory to the Father. Have mercy on us, O Lord, have mercy on us.

FIFTH STATION

Simon of Cyrene Helps Jesus to Carry His Cross

We adore you, O Christ, and we bless you, because by your holy cross you have redeemed the world.

SIMON OF CYRENE, you have the honor of helping Jesus carry his cross. Even if at first you draw back, his pathetic condition touches your heart with love and sympathy for him. Your strong hands hoist the cross and relieve Jesus of its crushing weight.

I have my own cross to carry. Help me to accept it willingly, so that I may complete "what is lacking in Christ's afflictions for the sake of his body, that is, the Church" (Col 1:24).

Jesus spent his life healing, teaching and helping others. When he needed help, a stranger had to assist him. That helps me to feel nearer to him, because in my sickness I am not always surrounded by my own friends and relatives, but have to accept the assistance of strangers. Jesus, when my illness makes me feel impatient and irritable, help me to be kind to those persons who serve my needs.

Our Father, Hail Mary, Glory to the Father.
Have mercy on us, O Lord, have mercy on us.

SIXTH STATION

Veronica Wipes the Face of Jesus

We adore you, O Christ, and we bless you, because by your holy cross you have redeemed the world.

Veronica, your loving kindness to our Savior consoles him during his way of the cross. To show compassion to Jesus, you fight your way through the crowds to reach him. You had the courage to ignore the soldiers who tried to block your way. Now having reached Jesus, with your own veil you wipe the blood and dirt from his face. So much blood has trickled down from the crown of thorns that Jesus can hardly see. You gently cleanse his face and Jesus looks at you with gratitude and love.

Help me to remember Jesus' words, "Just as you did it to one of the least of these...you did it to me" (Mt 25:40). Veronica, you had the good fortune of being able to minister to Jesus directly. I can minister to him by serving the needs of the people around me. If my illness prevents me from doing much, help me to remember that I can always pray for them.

Our Father, Hail Mary, Glory to the Father. Have mercy on us, O Lord, have mercy on us.

SEVENTH STATION

Jesus Falls the Second Time

We adore you, O Christ, and we bless you, because by your holy cross you have redeemed the world.

LORD JESUS, how can I console you for the suffering you endured? Weak and exhausted, you can hardly bear the heavy burden of the cross. You stumble and fall headlong onto the dusty road. With your hands bound you cannot break your fall, and your face grinds into the dirt and rocks. The mob surrounding you jeers and taunts you even more, adding insults to your physical sufferings.

Jesus, I offer you the lonely hours I spend in my sickness. I offer you all my pain to atone in part for the sins that caused you such terrible sufferings. I also pray for those who are struggling to recover from an addiction. Don't let them be discouraged if they fall, but give them the courage to continue the struggle.

Our Father, Hail Mary, Glory to the Father. Have mercy on us, O Lord, have mercy on us.

EIGHTH STATION

Jesus Consoles the Women of Jerusalem

We adore you, O Christ, and we bless you, because by your holy cross you have redeemed the world.

JESUS, now you are approaching the place of your crucifixion. Where are all the people you helped, those whom you comforted? You are alone in your agony; strangers and enemies surround you.

Nearby, a group of women are weeping for you. Their motherly hearts go out to you, and they try to offer whatever comfort they can. But instead of thinking of yourself, you offer them consolation: "Daughters of Jerusalem, do not weep for me, but weep for yourselves and for your children" (Lk 23:28).

Lord Jesus, keep me from falling into self-pity because of my illness. Don't let me crave sympathy from others, but like you, let me be the one to say a kind word and pray for those who have more pain than I do. Keep me close to you, Lord. I need you so much.

Our Father, Hail Mary, Glory to the Father. Have mercy on us, O Lord, have mercy on us.

NINTH STATION
JESUS FALLS THE THIRD TIME

We adore you, O Christ, and we bless you, because by your holy cross you have redeemed the world.

O MY WEARY LORD! This death march to Calvary keeps dragging on. What insults you have suffered! I can only marvel that you, the all-powerful God, consented to endure such agony. You have already suffered hour upon hour of torture. Your scourged body is racked with pain; the crown of thorns bites deeply into your skull. Your lips and throat burn with thirst and your whole body trembles with exhaustion.

Dear Jesus, with what words can I console you? I have offended you many times; now I ask your forgiveness. I grieve for my part in causing you to suffer and I offer you my heartfelt love and gratitude.

Our Father, Hail Mary, Glory to the Father. Have mercy on us, O Lord, have mercy on us.

TENTH STATION

Jesus Is Stripped of His Garments

We adore you, O Christ, and we bless you, because by your holy cross you have redeemed the world.

LORD JESUS, your journey is nearly over. Our redemption is being accomplished. What excruciating pain you must feel as the soldiers roughly rip off your garments, re-opening your wounds. Your sacred blood again flows for us sinners. The crowd is jeering and taunting you, adding more insults to your physical pain.

Lord, help me to bear patiently whatever pain my illness may cause me. Sometimes it seems like I can't endure it anymore. When that happens, help me to join my pain to yours. It consoles me to know that in this way I can contribute to the salvation of the world.

Our Father, Hail Mary, Glory to the Father. Have mercy on us, O Lord, have mercy on us.

ELEVENTH STATION

Jesus Is Nailed to the Cross

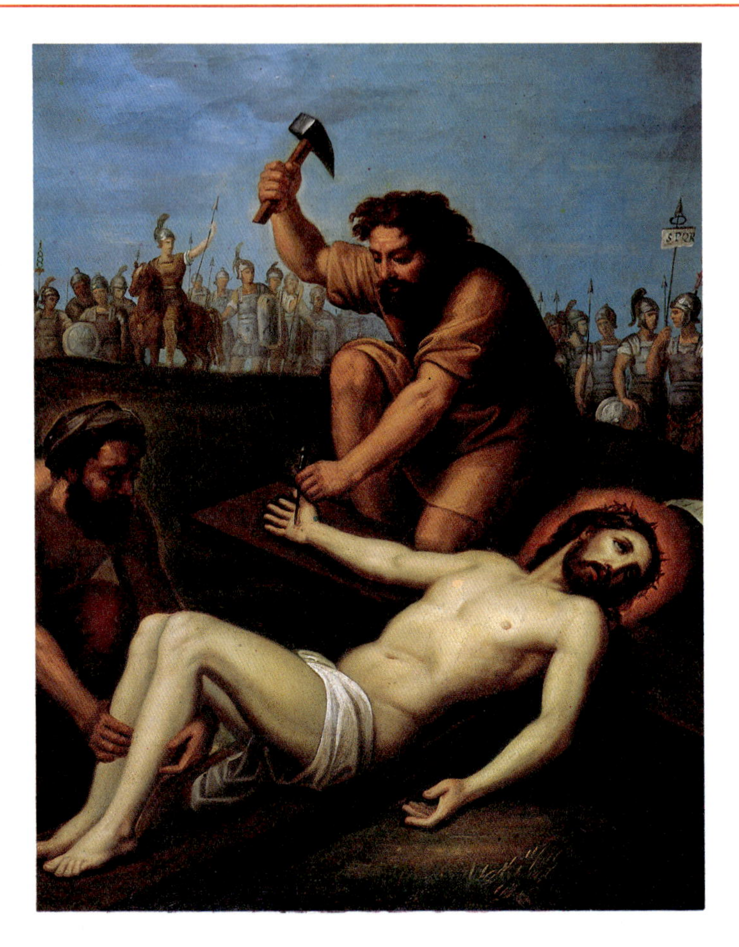

We adore you, O Christ, and we bless you, because by your holy cross you have redeemed the world.

MY LORD AND MY GOD, I adore you. How can I understand what you are suffering for us? The moment of your crucifixion has arrived. The soldiers wrench your hands and feet and pound the heavy nails in place. The splinters from the rough wood of the cross stab you at every movement. As they raise the cross and plunge it into the ground, the entire weight of your body makes tremors of agony pass through you. Your arms are nearly wrenched out of their sockets. Yet you have only mercy and forgiveness for your tormentors, praying "Father, forgive them; for they do not know what they are doing" (Lk 23:34). During these agonizing hours you will utter your seven last words. You will promise heaven to the good thief, and you will give us your blessed Mother.

Lord Jesus, help me to understand and appreciate your infinite love for me. I am sorry for my part in having offended you. I am grateful for all you have done and I love you with all my heart.

Our Father, Hail Mary, Glory to the Father. Have mercy on us, O Lord, have mercy on us.

TWELFTH STATION

JESUS DIES ON THE CROSS

We adore you, O Christ, and we bless you, because by your holy cross you have redeemed the world.

O MY LORD JESUS CHRIST, your suffering is nearly over now. You are hanging on the cross for us. I can hardly bear to think of your agony. You can barely breathe. Your whole body throbs with pain from the nails piercing your hands and feet. The crown of thorns cuts into your head and the bruises and wounds from your terrible scourging are causing you incredible pain. Your heart is broken with the anguish of a love rejected by your creatures. You even feel abandoned by your Father.

Lord Jesus, how you are suffering in that humiliating death! Help me to realize better what you endured out of love for me, and help me to respond with a heartfelt love. When I meditate on your passion and death, help me to understand that your sufferings were caused by sin. I am sorry for all my sins. Please give me the strength to avoid all deliberate sin. Keep me close to you always.

Our Father, Hail Mary, Glory to the Father. Have mercy on us, O Lord, have mercy on us.

THIRTEENTH STATION

Jesus Is Taken Down from the Cross

We adore you, O Christ, and we bless you, because by your holy cross you have redeemed the world.

LORD JESUS, I adore you, I love you and I offer you my thanks for the great work of redemption you have just completed. Now your suffering is ended. One of the soldiers pierces your side with a spear, and blood and water flowed out. Your friends come and take your body down from the cross. Your Mother's heart breaks at the sight of her dead son, but she knows that you have accomplished your mission.

My sickness often causes me to feel pain. Help me not to complain about it, but to know how to offer everything to you with a spirit of love. Please accept my sufferings and join them to yours, and make them fruitful for the salvation of the world.

Our Father, Hail Mary, Glory to the Father.
Have mercy on us, O Lord, have mercy on us.

FOURTEENTH STATION

JESUS IS BURIED IN THE TOMB

We adore you, O Christ, and we bless you, because by your holy cross you have redeemed the world.

LORD JESUS, you are so poor that you have to be buried in a borrowed tomb. With a spirit of generosity, Joseph of Arimathea gives you his tomb. He and the holy women hastily prepare your body for burial. The Sabbath is almost upon them. They accompany your body to the grave and begin to mourn.

Though you have finished your earthly life, you have left us a precious legacy: your Mother, and the holy sacrifice of the Mass. You gave Mary to John as his mother, and through him, you gave her to all of us. In the Mass you have left us a memorial of the sacrifice of the cross. Through the Mass we receive the fruits of your sacrifice. In Holy Communion we receive your Body and Blood, and are intimately united with you.

If my sickness prevents me from participating in Mass as often as I would like, help me to join in spirit with the Masses that are being offered throughout the world. I love you, Jesus, with all my heart and I am sorry for all my sins. I desire to receive you in Holy Communion, and if I cannot receive you sacramentally, please come spiritually into my soul.

Our Father, Hail Mary, Glory to the Father. Have mercy on us, O Lord, have mercy on us.

Concluding Prayer

Lord Jesus, your death was not a defeat. It was a victory. You conquered sin and broke the power of the devil. On Easter Sunday you rose from the dead. I believe that one day I too will rise to a new life with you. As St. Paul says, "Christ has been raised from the dead, the first fruits of those who have died" (1 Cor 15:20). Help me to always live with this hope, and never to be discouraged by my sickness and weakness. I thank you for the gift of your love and your grace. Keep it always alive in me. *Amen.*